A BOOK INSPIRED BY DR. FESTUS ADEYEYE

I0081578

THE
CAMELS
ARE COMING

Building Inner Resilience Through Divine and Human Connections

A Powerful guide to discovering resilience, faith, and the human connections that carry us through life's deserts.

OLU OJEIKERE

Copyright © 2025 by **Olu Ojeikere**

Printed in the United States of America. All rights reserved solely by the author. No part of this book may be reproduced in any form without the written permission of the author. Unless otherwise indicated, Bible quotations are taken from the Holy Bible, New Living Translation. Copyright © 1996, 2004, 2007, 2013 by Tyndale House Foundation. Used by permission of Tyndale House Publishers, Inc., Carol Stream, Illinois 60188. All rights reserved.

ISBN 13: 978-1-7343991-6-5

PUBLISHED BY: Platform for Success Press
+1 917 826 3566, info@pacetas.com

ORDERING INFORMATION:
To order this book, please write to:

Olu Ojeikere
121-12 Milburn Street,
Springfield Gardens, NY 11413
E-mail: Oluojeikere@yahoo.com
www.oluojeikere.com

DEDICATION

To all those who have been *Camels* to me and to countless others; carriers of burdens, bearers of hope, and quiet companions through the wilderness of life, this work is a tribute to your strength and your grace.

To my immediate family and my beloved siblings, thank you for walking beside me through every season, for believing in the vision long before it took form, and for being an unshakable part of this journey toward fulfilling my purpose.

And lastly, to my bosom brother, Innocent Okonji; thank you for once again declaring that this book could indeed be written. Your confidence lit the spark that became these pages.

With deep gratitude and love.

TABLE OF CONTENTS

FOREWORD
Dr. Festus Adeyeye

Success in life is truly a collaboration of our personal determination and the support of the wonderful people around us. It blossoms when we tap into our inner strength while embracing both divine guidance and meaningful connections—what I like to call "destiny partnerships."

In The Camels Are Coming: Building Resilience Through Human and Divine Connection, Pastor Olu Ojeikere brilliantly reveals this vital truth: while Faith can move mountains, it's our persistence and the nurturing of our relationships that create a solid foundation for our journeys. He skillfully blends the relentless pursuit of our dreams with the grace that emerges from divine assistance.

This book is not just a guide; it's a transformative journey that will bolster your commitment, deepen your relationships, and reignite your belief in endless possibilities. As you delve into its pages, you'll uncover invaluable insights, feel inspired, and unlock the empowerment necessary to make remarkable strides toward fulfilling your destiny. Join us on this transformative journey—your future awaits!

ACKNOWLEDGMENT

This work was inspired by the profound message **"The Camels Are Coming"** delivered by **Dr. Festus Adeyeye**, whose words ignited the vision for this book.

With gratitude and honor, I acknowledge his wisdom and spiritual insight, which continue to guide and strengthen countless lives.

May every reader find in these pages the same divine encouragement that first stirred this message within my heart.

— **Olu Ojeikere**

PREFACE

Strength comes through connection. It is one of life's quiet miracles that nothing stands alone. Every living thing, no matter how self-sufficient it appears, draws strength from something beyond itself. The tallest tree reaches toward the sun, the floating bird rides on the wind. Even the human soul—brave, intelligent, determined—cannot thrive in isolation.

At the heart of every meaningful life is **connection**. Yet, beneath every connection lies something deeper: **resilience**—the inner strength that enables us to endure, adapt, and keep walking through life's deserts.

This book, inspired by *Dr. Festus Adeyeye's Camels Are Coming* message, explores that truth. It paints a vivid picture of what happens when divine help and human relationships intersect. The "Camels" in our lives are not simply people who appear to assist us; they are living symbols of grace and endurance—messengers who carry strength to weary travelers.

But the greater revelation is this: We are not only meant to receive help—we are called to become Camels ourselves. To embody traits that make life possible for others—**resilience, patience, adaptability,**

endurance, resourcefulness, strength, loyalty, and calmness—and in doing so, become bridges of hope in a world that often feels like a wilderness.

In these pages, you'll find reflections and stories drawn from both spiritual and everyday life. You'll discover how to cultivate the quiet power that sustains great friendships, strong families, enduring Faith, and purposeful leadership. The Camels are coming is not a book about surviving the desert; it is a guide to thriving within it—drawing strength from God, wisdom from experience, and courage from community.

Each chapter offers lessons from nature and humanity—reminding us that resilience is not an inherited trait; it is a cultivated strength. And that every person, regardless of background or belief, is capable of becoming a source of empowerment for others. May this book renew your confidence that the desert is not the end of the story; help is always on the way. Your Camels are coming—and perhaps, you are one of them.

CHAPTER ONE

STRENGTH IN CONNECTION

Meeting The Camels In Your Life

"Sometimes our light goes out but is blown again into instant flame by an encounter with another human being."
— Albert Schweitzer.

Every person walking this earth has known a desert moment—a season of weariness, uncertainty, or loss. In those moments, strength often comes from people: a friend who listens, a mentor who guides, a stranger who shows unexpected kindness. These are the *Camels* of life—helpers who carry hope across the barren places of our journey.

Camels are not glamorous creatures, but they are steady, enduring, and faithful. They survive heat, hunger, and hardship. They symbolize the kind of people who keep showing up when life becomes too heavy to carry alone.

The message of this book begins here: **the power of connection is not merely relational, it is transformational.** The people who cross our paths are often divine appointments meant to strengthen our inner life.

The Hidden Network of Help

We often mistake resilience for self-reliance, but no one is self-made. Behind every success story is a web of unseen support, a teacher, a parent, a colleague, a friend. Every strong person once leaned on another's strength. Connection is how resilience multiplies.

In spiritual terms, God rarely works in isolation. His help often arrives through people "Camels" who carry encouragement, wisdom, and provision. In psychological terms, this is called *social resilience*: the ability to endure hardship through supportive relationships. Whether divine or human, connection strengthens us from the inside out.

Think of your own journey. Who stood beside you when hope was low?

Who believed in you when you could not believe in yourself? Those people were not coincidences; they were carriers of strength sent to ensure you reached the next stage of your purpose.

Resilience Shared Is Strength Multiplied

Camels teach us that strength is meant to be shared. In the desert, survival depends not on speed but on endurance. One camel kneels so the traveler can climb; another carries water for the group. Similarly, the strongest among us are those who use their resilience to empower others.

True connection is never one-sided. It transforms both the giver and the receiver. When someone helps you through a storm, their strength becomes your seed of endurance. And when you, in turn, help someone else, resilience flows through you to them, a demonstration of how strength circulates in the human family— quietly, faithfully, eternally.

Connection as a Spiritual and Practical Force

For the person of Faith, connection reveals divine design: *two are better than one, for they have a good reward for their labor* (Ecclesiastes 4:9).

But even beyond Faith, life proves that isolation weakens and collaboration strengthens. Psychologists confirm what Scripture has long declared relationships are among the greatest predictors of emotional stability and longevity.

To walk with others is to share resilience. To journey alone is to risk collapse under the heat of life's sun.

Becoming the Camel

Every person reading this book has the potential to be someone's Camel, to lift, to encourage, and to carry. You may not have great wealth or titles, but if you have character, empathy, and consistency, you have strength enough to sustain another soul.

Ask yourself:

- Who has been a Camel in my life?
- Who am I being a Camel right now?

- How can I strengthen others through my journey?

The Call to Walk Together

Life's deserts are long, but no one was created to walk them alone.

The message of *The Camels Are Coming* is not only about finding help, but it's about becoming help. It's about discovering that your trials have trained you to carry others, that your strength was not meant to end with you.

Connection gives birth to resilience, and resilience transforms connection into a legacy. So, as you read on, remember: The desert may be vast, but you are never without help. The Camels are coming—and if you listen closely, you may hear the camels' footsteps already.

CHAPTER TWO

RESILIENCE

The Power to Rise Again

"It's not the strongest of the species that survives, nor the most intelligent, but the one most responsive to change."
— Charles Darwin.

There are moments in life when the journey feels like a desert—dry, unending, and unkind. The winds of disappointment whip against us, and the horizon offers no promise of quick relief. In these seasons, the most valuable quality is not comfort or speed, it is **resilience**, the quiet strength to keep moving forward when everything else tells you to stop.

Resilience is not the absence of struggle. It is the ability to bend but not break, to endure without becoming bitter, to fall and rise again with renewed perspective. The "Camels" in our lives embody this beautifully. They stand as living metaphors for grace under pressure—steady helpers who remind us that even in the harshest conditions, survival is possible, and growth is inevitable.

The Desert as a Teacher

Camels are designed for endurance. They can go days without water, store energy in their humps, and withstand intense heat and cold. Every feature of their body is built to survive what others cannot. Their design is not accidental—it is purposeful. Likewise, our challenges are not meant to destroy us but to develop our inner design for resilience.

The desert of life teaches lessons that comfort never can:

- You learn what truly matters.
- You discover strength you didn't know you had.
- You realize that growth often hides inside hardship.

When life strips away what's easy, what remains is what's essential—and resilience becomes your anchor.

The Hidden Strength Within

Resilience is more than endurance; it's transformation. It doesn't merely help you return to who you were before hardship—it refines you into someone wiser, humbler, and stronger. Each time you rise from a setback, your inner reserves deepen. Like a camel that drinks deeply before a long journey, you store strength that will sustain you in the next challenge.

For people of Faith, this strength is not self-generated. It flows from divine connection—God's presence that anchors us when everything else shakes. Yet even outside the language of Faith, resilience is a universal virtue. It is the courage to hope again after loss, to trust again after betrayal, to rebuild again after ruin.

A Story of Quiet Strength

Rosa worked as a nurse during one of the most chaotic health crises in her city's history. Every day, she faced exhaustion, fear, and uncertainty. Supplies ran low, shifts grew longer, and emotions ran high. Yet through it all, she greeted her patients with calm assurance.

Her colleagues leaned on her; her presence steadied them. She never pretended the situation was easy, but she carried herself with quiet resolve.

When asked how she managed, she replied, *"I remember why I'm here."*

Rosa's resilience didn't erase her challenges, it redefined them.

Her strength became a refuge for others. In her steadiness, people found peace. That is the secret of resilient Camels: they don't just survive; they carry others safely through their storm.

Resilience as a Shared Gift

When you become resilient, your strength no longer serves you alone, it becomes a gift to others. A parent's calm becomes a child's security. A leader's stability becomes a team's confidence. A friend's Faith becomes another's courage to keep going.

The strongest people are not those who never fall; they are those who rise and lift others as they stand.

The Apostle Paul wrote, *"We are troubled on every side, yet not distressed; perplexed, but not in despair"* (2 Corinthians 4:8). That's not denial—it's divine endurance. Resilience turns trials into testimonies and pressure into power.

Building Resilience

Resilience is not an accident of personality—it is a practice of perspective. It grows every time we choose hope over fear and perseverance over surrender.

Here are principles that strengthen the resilient spirit:

1. **Prepare Before the Storm**: Camels store water before they cross the desert. Likewise, build your inner reserves through prayer, reflection, and learning before a crisis comes. Preparation builds stability.
2. **Anchor Yourself in Purpose**: People who know *why* they're walking can endure almost anyhow. Remember your calling, your values, your reason to keep going.
3. **Stay Connected**: Resilient people draw from their network of support. Isolation weakens resolve, but connection multiplies strength. Don't journey alone.
4. **Reframe Adversity**: Instead of asking "Why me?" ask "What is this teaching me?" Every hardship carries hidden wisdom.
5. **Serve Others Through Your Struggle**: Helping someone else in your storm often gives your own meaning to your own pain. Your experience becomes someone else's encouragement.

When Resilience Meets Faith

In Faith, resilience is not just survival, it is spiritual victory.

It's what happens when your human endurance meets divine strength. Scripture reminds us that *"those who wait upon the Lord shall renew their strength"* (Isaiah 40:31). Waiting here doesn't mean passivity, it means inner renewal, quiet confidence that the One who called you is also carrying you.

When you trust that your desert has purpose, the heat can no longer defeat you, it becomes part of your preparation.

Becoming a Resilient Camel

You may not realize it, but someone is watching how you handle your storms.

Your calmness under fire, your persistence in adversity, your decision to keep loving and giving—these inspire others to believe that they, too, can rise again.

Camels are not beautiful, but they are indispensable. Their greatness is in their steady faithfulness, their quiet strength. In the same way, your resilience may not attract applause, but it will leave an unshakable mark on the lives of those you carry.

Reflection

- What adversity in your life taught you the most about resilience?
- Who has carried you through your toughest desert?
- How can your story of endurance strengthen someone else?

Closing Thought

Resilience is the heartbeat of life's journey. It transforms suffering into wisdom and hardship into strength. The desert may be fierce, but the resilient traveler is fiercer still.

And just as camels walk with quiet purpose toward the horizon, so too must we be steady, enduring, and full of Faith that better days are ahead. Because resilience is not just about surviving; it's about becoming someone others can lean on when their strength runs dry. That's the power of a Camel heart.

CHAPTER THREE

PATIENCE

The Strength of Slow Progress

> *"Patience is bitter, but its fruit is sweet."*
> — Jean-Jacques Rousseau

In a world that celebrates speed, patience can feel like weakness. We live in an age of instant downloads, fast food, and next-day delivery. Yet, the most meaningful transformations in life—character, healing, purpose, relationships—require time. Patience is not about waiting passively; it's about enduring actively. It's the calm strength to trust the process when results are not immediate.

Camels embody this perfectly. They are never in a hurry, yet they always arrive. Step by step, they cross impossible distances under the burning sun, carrying both their burdens and those who depend on them. Their pace may seem slow, but it is steady—and in the desert, steady is what survives.

Patience is the soul's strength to endure without giving up, and it's one of the defining marks of a resilient life.

Patience: The Power Behind Progress

Patience is not a lack of ambition. It's the discipline to stay on the course when progress seems invisible. The impatient may begin with passion, but the patient finishes with purpose.

The desert of life often stretches farther than we expect. In those long seasons, patience becomes the bridge between promise and fulfillment. The ability to keep walking when nothing seems to change is proof of inner resilience.

Camels understand this rhythm. They conserve energy, regulate pace, and move forward deliberately. They teach us that the secret to finishing the journey isn't in speed, but in *consistency*—in refusing to stop.

A Story of Transformative Patience

Ethan, a music teacher in an inner-city neighborhood, spent years working with students who had little interest in learning. Many faced family challenges, poverty, and self-doubt. Progress was painfully slow. But Ethan kept showing up. He celebrated small wins, repeated lessons with grace, and never lost Faith in their potential.

Years later, one of his former students returned as a successful orchestra director. When asked what had changed his life, he said, "My teacher believed in me long before I believed in myself."

Ethan's patience wasn't passive—it was purposeful endurance. He understood what every Camel knows: transformation takes time. The journey that changes people rarely happens overnight.

The Strength of Stillness

Patience is a strength forged in stillness. It's what allows us to remain peaceful while everything inside us screams for action. When we learn to wait well, we grow wiser, stronger, and more discerning. Impatience makes us reactive; patience makes us resilient.

Faith teaches this truth beautifully. Abraham waited decades for a promise to unfold. Joseph waited in prison before he was appointed ruler of the palace. Jesus waited in obscurity before his public ministry began. Their stories remind us that waiting time is not wasted time, it's preparation time.

In the same way, life uses waiting to stretch our capacity. The process that seems slow is often where strength is formed.

Why Patience Is a Form of Power

1. **It Builds Perspective**: Patience helps us see beyond the moment. What feels like a delay often hides divine design.
2. **It Protects Energy**: Like camels conserving strength, patience prevents emotional burnout.
3. **It Deepens Trust**: When we can't control outcomes, patience teaches us to trust God, people, and the process.
4. **It Strengthens Relationships**: Patience allows us to love imperfect people as they grow.
5. **It Multiplies Wisdom**: The patient person doesn't rush decisions; they discern timing—and timing is everything.

Patience in a Culture of Urgency

Our generation has confused movement with progress. We equate activity with accomplishment. But real growth, emotional, spiritual, professional—takes time. The seed doesn't rush to become a tree; it rests in darkness until it's ready to emerge.

Camels do not compete with the wind; they adapt to its rhythm. Likewise, patient people move in step with wisdom, not pressure. They understand that every season has its appointed time and that maturity cannot be microwaved.

Patience is not slowness—it's strength with direction.

A Modern Story of Enduring Faith

Sophia, a social worker, once cared for a foster child named Malik— a boy hardened by rejection and distrust. His progress was painfully slow. Many believed he would never open up. But Sophia stayed— day after day, year after year—advocating for him, believing in him, listening even when he lashed out.

Eventually, Malik found healing. Years later, at his graduation, he thanked her publicly: "You stayed when everyone else left."

Sophia's patience didn't just change Malik—it shaped his future. Her endurance permitted him to trust again. That's what patient people do: they carry others through the long journey of becoming.

The Spiritual Foundation of Patience

Faith gives patience a deeper anchor. The believer's patience is rooted in trust that God is at work even when progress is unseen. The

Scriptures remind us that *"those who wait upon the Lord shall renew their strength"* (Isaiah 40:31). Waiting, then, is not passive; it's spiritual training.

For the person without a faith label, the principle still holds patience is power under control. It is the art of steady progress. It is the ability to trust timing more than impulse—to walk in peace rather than panic.

How to Cultivate Patience

1. **Embrace Process, Not Just Results:** Focus on growth, not speed. Progress happens with one faithful step at a time.
2. **Celebrate Small Victories**: Every step forward deserves gratitude. The desert is crossed in increments.
3. **Practice Presence**: Don't live so far in the future that you miss the blessings of now.
4. **Release Control**: Let go of the illusion that everything must happen on your schedule.
5. **Wait With Purpose**: Use waiting seasons to prepare, pray, and refine your character.

Becoming a Patient Camel

To be patient is to carry hope without haste. It's about keeping walking when the horizon feels distant and believing that every step counts.

Camels are patient not because they have no choice, but because they have learned that endurance preserves strength. They don't stop for every discomfort or storm; they move with rhythm, grace, and trust.

In the same way, patience transforms your waiting seasons into sacred ground. Every delay becomes development. Every detour becomes a discovery. Every long road builds your inner capacity to carry more tomorrow than you could today.

Reflection

- What area of your life requires you to practice patience right now?
- How has impatience robbed you of peace or progress in the past?
- Who needs your patience today—someone growing, healing, or finding their way?

Closing Thought

Patience is not about how long you wait—it's about how well you wait.

It's the quiet courage to keep trusting when nothing seems to move, the steady heart that refuses to quit, and the calm conviction that time is working for you, not against you.

Like the Camel crossing endless sand, the patient soul keeps walking toward the promise. Because even in silence, progress is happening step by step, day by day. And when the journey finally opens into an oasis, you'll look back and see that patience was not the delay, it was the very path to strength.

CHAPTER FOUR

ADAPTABILITY
Thriving in Shifting Sands

> *"All failure is failure to adapt; all success is successful adaptation."*
> — Max McKeown

The desert changes without warning. One day, it is calm and bright; the next, a sandstorm rises without mercy. The travelers who survive are not necessarily the strongest but the most adaptable. Camels thrive in these unpredictable conditions because they are built to adapt. Their bodies shift with temperature, their pace matches the terrain, and their instincts lead them through danger without panic.

In the same way, life requires us to bend without breaking. Adaptability is the art of stability in motion—the quiet intelligence that allows us to stay true to our purpose while changing our approach. It is not a compromise; it is capacity. And it is one of the purest forms of resilience.

When Life Shifts Beneath You

Change comes for everyone. Sometimes it arrives as an opportunity, other times as a disruption. Careers evolve; relationships shift, seasons end, and new ones begin. The ability to thrive amid change determines whether we merely survive life or grow through it.

Adaptability doesn't mean we stop feeling the discomfort of transition. It means we learn how to move through it with grace. We stop fighting the wind and instead learn to sail with it.

Camels do not curse the heat or the cold—they respond to it. They lower their heart rate in intense heat and draw on stored reserves when food is scarce. Every trait is a reminder that wisdom is not about control; it's about alignment—the willingness to work with what is, not against it.

A Story of Creative Adjustment

When the global pandemic shut down cities across the world, a small family bakery called *The Parker Café* faced extinction. Overnight, their daily customers vanished, and their income dropped to zero. But instead of giving up, they adapted.

They moved their business online, began offering doorstep deliveries, and started baking comfort loaves for hospitals and shelters. What started as survival became their most impactful season yet—the community rallied, new customers emerged, and their story spread as an example of courage in crisis.

Adaptability turned a setback into an opportunity for service. Like the desert traveler adjusting to a new path, the Parkers discovered that flexibility is often the birthplace of resilience.

Adaptability as Emotional Strength

Change isn't just external, it's emotional. Adaptable people have learned to navigate internal shifts with maturity. They understand that stability is not the absence of change, but the ability to stay grounded through it.

Emotionally adaptable people:

- Listen more than they react.
- Reframe challenges as invitations to grow.
- Stay hopeful when outcomes are uncertain.
- Ask better questions instead of assigning blame.
- Accept that discomfort is part of progress.

Adaptability is not about pretending everything is fine, it's about finding strength in what remains when things are not.

Lessons from Faith and Nature

In Scripture, adaptability is woven into the stories of those who fulfilled purpose under pressure. Joseph was adaptable—thrown into a pit, sold into slavery, then imprisoned—yet each environment revealed a new skill, preparing him for leadership in Egypt. Ruth was adaptable leaving her homeland to embrace a new faith and family, finding destiny where she least expected it.

God often leads through seasons of change because purpose requires flexibility. The soil must be broken before it can receive seed; the seed must die before it can grow. Adaptability is that sacred breaking—what feels like disruption is often preparation.

In nature, every living thing that thrives learns to adapt. Trees bend with the wind, rivers carve new paths, and even stars shift with the rhythm of time. The lesson is simple: what refuses to adapt eventually fades.

Building the Muscle of Adaptability

Adaptability is not an inherited talent; it's a mindset you can develop.

1. Embrace Change Instead of Resisting It: Change is uncomfortable because it demands movement. But the sooner you embrace it; the sooner you regain control of your direction.

2. Reframe Your Perspective: Ask not, "Why is this happening to me?" but "What is this preparing me for?" Every shift has a lesson attached.

3. Strengthen Your Emotional Agility: Practice calm reflection before reaction. Take a breath before you respond. This pause is where wisdom is born.

4. Stay Curious: Curiosity disarms fear. The person who keeps learning will always find a way to adjust.

5. Nurture Your Network: The more connected you are, the more resources you have when change comes. Relationships are bridges during seasons of transition.

6. Keep Your Purpose in Sight: Adaptability never means abandoning your purpose. It means adjusting your methods while staying faithful to your mission.

A Story of Transformative Leadership

Maria became the principal of a struggling high school. The students were disillusioned, teachers were burnt out, and the community had lost trust. Many leaders before her had failed because they clung to old systems. Maria chose a different path.

She listened first. She met with students and parents, observed teachers, and reimagined the schedule to fit her community's needs. She implemented mentorship programs, flexible class hours, and creative learning incentives. Within two years, the school's dropout rate plummeted.

Maria didn't succeed because she was the smartest—she succeeded because she was the most adaptable. She refused to force progress through rigid tradition; she shaped tradition to serve progress.

Adaptability in Relationships

Just as in leadership, adaptability sustains relationships. No person remains the same forever. Friends evolve, spouses grow, children change, and colleagues shift priorities. Loving someone long-term is to adapt with them—to keep learning who they're becoming instead of holding onto who they were.

Rigid expectations fracture the connection. Adaptability keeps relationships alive.

The strongest marriages, friendships, and teams aren't those that avoid change but those that grow through it together.

Spiritual Adaptability: The Gift of Surrender

Spiritually, adaptability is the courage to say, "Lord, not my way, but yours."

It's trusting in divine timing when plans unravel and believing that redirection is still destiny. Sometimes, God shifts your path not to punish you, but to position you.

When life changes suddenly, the adaptable believer asks, *"What is God doing here that I cannot yet see?"* That posture turns fear into Faith and uncertainty into worship.

Becoming an Adaptable Camel

To be a Camel is to be both steady and flexible—to carry purpose with poise, even when the terrain shifts beneath your feet. Camels do not panic in sandstorms; they kneel, wait, and rise when the storm passes. That posture is wisdom. It is surrender without defeat, Faith without fear.

Adaptability allows you to adjust your methods without losing your mission—to pause without giving up, to wait without wandering off course. When you master this trait, you become a stabilizing presence in others' lives.

People will draw courage from your calmness, clarity from your composure, and hope from your ability to adapt with grace.

Reflection

- What recent change has challenged your adaptability?
- How might flexibility—not resistance—help you grow through it?
- Who in your life needs encouragement to adapt rather than give up?

Closing Thought

Life's desert will always change shape. The wind will shift, the sands will move, and familiar paths will disappear. But those who adapt—those who bend without breaking—will always find a way forward.

Adaptability doesn't just help you survive storms; it teaches you to thrive in them.

It makes you a Camel—steady in purpose, flexible in process, and strong enough to carry others through their shifting sands. Because the truth is simple: the desert will change, but your destiny will not.

CHAPTER FIVE

ENDURANCE
The Gift of Staying Power

> *"With patience and endurance, even the weakest thread can pierce the strongest stone."*
> — Chinese Proverb.

Suppose resilience is the ability to rise again, and adaptability is the skill to shift with change. In that case, endurance is the grace to keep going—again and again, without losing heart.

Endurance is not about speed or energy; it's about faithfulness. It is the decision to remain when every instinct says to walk away. It is the courage to continue walking through life's desert, mile after mile, trusting that each step still matters.

Camels are the perfect picture of endurance. They are not celebrated for beauty or brilliance, but for one extraordinary gift: they stay. They move slowly but steadily, carrying heavy loads across unforgiving terrain, refusing to stop until they reach their destination.

Endurance is love that refuses to quit.

The Strength of Staying

In a world addicted to instant success and quick rewards, endurance is becoming a lost art. We chase novelty but abandon consistency. We begin with fire but end with fatigue. Yet the truth is timeless, anything that lasts is built on endurance.

Faith, marriage, purpose, leadership, legacy—none survive without it.

Camels remind us that progress is not always visible. They walk in silence through miles of sameness before an oasis appears. Their strength lies in rhythm, not rush. In the same way, endurance is not glamorous, but it is powerful. It builds depth, trust, and lasting impact.

A Story of Unwavering Commitment

Liam was born prematurely, weighing less than two pounds. Doctors said survival was uncertain, and even if he lived, he might never walk or speak normally. His mother, Rachel, chose a different response—she endured.

She spent sleepless nights in hospital corridors, learned medical routines, and built her life around Liam's care. For years, she drove to appointments, prayed through setbacks, and celebrated the smallest victories.

Years later, Liam walked across his graduation stage, healthy and full of promise. When asked how she kept going, Rachel smiled and said, *"Love learns to stay."*

That's endurance. Not heroism. Not perfection. Just love that refuses to stop showing up.

Endurance: The Unseen Power

Endurance doesn't always look like triumph. Sometimes it looks like quiet perseverance, staying faithful in a job that tests your patience, continuing to love a difficult child, or holding onto Faith when answers don't come.

Camels do not run in storms; they kneel and wait. They rest, conserve strength, and rise again when the wind settles. That's not weakness; that's wisdom.

Likewise, endurance doesn't mean endless motion—it means purposeful persistence. It knows when to press forward and when to pause to regain strength. Endurance teaches us that the greatest victories often come after long seasons of silence.

Endurance in Faith and Life

Scripture is filled with people who discovered the power of endurance:

- **Noah** endured ridicule while building something no one had ever seen.
- **Job** endured suffering without losing his reverence for God.

- **Paul** endured persecution with the conviction that the purpose was greater than pain.

The Bible tells us, *"Let us not grow weary in doing good, for in due season we shall reap, if we do not give up."* (Galatians 6:9)

Endurance is what bridge promises and fulfillment. It transforms hope into reality. Even outside Faith, history proves the same truth—enduring hearts shape the world. Scientists, artists, teachers, caregivers—all change lives through consistency, not convenience.

Building Endurance: Habits of Those Who Stay

1. **Pace Yourself**: Endurance is not sprinting; it's setting a rhythm you can sustain. Camels survive because they move with wisdom, not exhaustion.
2. **Rest Strategically**: Rest is not quitting. It's recharging for longevity.
3. Even the most committed must pause to recover.
4. **Celebrate Small Wins**: Every completed step deserves gratitude. Small victories fuel long journeys.
5. **Hold Your 'Why' Close**: Purpose is the oxygen of endurance. When your 'why' is strong, you can survive almost any 'how.'
6. **Lean on Others**: Camels travel in caravans for a reason—community sustains endurance. Don't journey alone.
7. **Choose Faith Over Feelings**: Feelings fluctuate; faith anchors. Trust that perseverance produces results even when emotions waver.

The Unsung Heroes of Endurance

Look around, and you'll see them everywhere, nurses who keep serving through exhaustion, teachers who invest in struggling students, pastors who preach through personal storms, parents who keep on believing in a prodigal child.

They are the quiet Camels of our world—steady, consistent, uncelebrated, yet essential. Their strength is measured not by speed but by staying power. Their legacy is not written in headlines but in the hearts, they've carried across deserts.

A Modern Example: The Steadfast Neighbor

During a city flood, an older man named Thomas spent three days ferrying neighbors to safety in his small canoe. When volunteers offered to take over, he smiled and said, "I've lived here my whole life. I'll leave when the last person does."

No cameras, no applause—just a man who refused to quit until the work was done. Endurance is like that. It doesn't always roar; sometimes it simply refuses to stop.

When Endurance Becomes Legacy

The fruit of endurance often appears long after the journey ends. A teacher's patience produces generations of leaders. A mother's prayers outlive her years. A mentor's steady encouragement reshapes destiny.

Camels never boast about how far they've come, but their tracks mark the path for others to follow. Every act of endurance adds to your legacy—a living testimony that strength is not proven by how loud you start, but by how long you last.

Becoming an Enduring Camel

To be an enduring Camel is to live with faithful persistence. It's to show up when the feeling fades, to walk by principle rather than passion, and to love without expiration.

Endurance is not perfection; it's perseverance. It's what transforms ordinary lives into extraordinary examples of Faith, service, and love.

When you keep going, others keep on believing. When you stay, others find the courage to remain. When you endure, you make the invisible visible—you make Faith tangible.

Reflection

- Where in your life are you being called to *stay* when everything in you want to leave?
- Who around you need your endurance as a model of faithfulness?
- What small habit can you begin today to build long-term strength?

Closing Thought

The desert is long, but it's not endless. The heat is real, but so is the destination. Endurance doesn't promise an easy road, it promises a meaningful one. So, keep walking. Rest when you must. Rise when it's time because the finish line belongs not to the fastest, but to the faithful. And when your journey is done, you will discover that endurance wasn't just the key to reaching the oasis—it was the very thing that made you stronger along the way.

CHAPTER SIX

RESOURCEFULNESS
Finding Strength in What You Have

> *"Do what you can, with what you have, where you are."*
> — Theodore Roosevelt

The desert is an unforgiving place. There are no guarantees of comfort or abundance. Yet, some travelers thrive where others faint—not because they have more, but because they use what they have more wisely.

Camels embody this truth with quiet brilliance. They waste nothing. Their design is a master class in efficiency—storing fat in their humps for energy, adjusting body temperature to conserve water, and walking steadily through terrain that defeats most animals.

This resourcefulness: the ability to create possibilities out of limitations.

It's not having everything you want; it's seeing everything you have as enough to begin. Resourcefulness turns scarcity into strength and challenge into creativity.

The Art of Making Much Out of Little

Life rarely gives us perfect conditions. Dreams are often born in lack, ideas in tension, and breakthroughs in discomfort. Resourceful people understand this. They stop waiting for the ideal and start working with the real.

Camels never wish for rivers, they make the desert work for them. They adapt to their environment and draw on their inner reserves to survive. Likewise, those who thrive in life learn to use their talents, relationships, time, and opportunities with vision and gratitude.

The secret of resourcefulness is perspective. It's not about what's missing, it's about what's already within reach.

A Story of Courageous Creativity

During World War II, a young woman named Miep Gies risked her life to shelter Anne Frank and her family. With food scarce and danger ever-present, she became a lifeline—smuggling supplies, forging ration cards, and building trust with local shopkeepers.

She had little to offer but used everything she could. Her courage, cleverness, and compassion saved lives. When the family was eventually discovered, Miep found and preserved Anne's diary— ensuring the world would hear a young girl's story of hope.

Miep didn't wait for resources; she became resourceful. Her ingenuity under pressure changed history.

The Power of Resourcefulness in Daily Life

You don't need a crisis to practice creativity. Every day brings opportunities to stretch what you have:

- A single encouraging word can restore someone's confidence.
- A small idea, pursued faithfully, can grow into a thriving enterprise.
- A moment of empathy can heal what money cannot.

Resourcefulness is a mindset, not a material condition. It begins when you stop complaining about lack and start *creating* with what you already possess.

The greatest innovators, leaders, and helpers didn't begin with abundance; they began with belief. They saw limitations as an invitation.

Faith and Resourcefulness: The Divine Equation

Throughout Scripture, God's power often revealed itself through scarcity.

Moses had only one staff, yet it parted the seas. David had only a sling, yet it toppled a giant. A widow had only a jar of oil, yet it filled many vessels. A boy had five loaves and two fish, yet they fed thousands.

In every case, God didn't add something new; He multiplied what was already there. That's the beauty of divine resourcefulness—God works best through what seems small, inadequate, or ordinary.

Faith and creativity are partners. When you trust that what you have is enough for God to use, miracles begin.

A Modern Example: The Seed of a Movement

In Kenya, Wangari Maathai noticed that her community's farmland was eroding due to deforestation. With no money or government support, she started planting trees in her own backyard. That small act of Faith grew into the *Green Belt Movement*, which has since planted over fifty million trees and empowered thousands of women.

Her resourcefulness didn't just restore the land—it restored dignity and hope.

She turned scarcity into sustainability and pain into purpose.

How to Cultivate Resourcefulness

1. Reframe Limitations as Opportunities: Every challenge is a disguised classroom. Ask, *what can I do with what I have right now?*

2. Start Where You Are: Don't wait for the perfect condition. Progress is born in motion, not hesitation.

3. Expand Through Learning: The more you know, the more options you create. Stay curious; resourcefulness grows with wisdom.

4. Build Relationships as Resources: People are often the greatest assets. Collaboration multiplies capacity.

5. Practice Gratitude: Gratitude opens your eyes to abundance. It shifts focus from what's lacking to what's available.

6. Simplify and Strategize: Cut out what drains energy. Resourcefulness thrives in clarity, not clutter.

Resourcefulness and Emotional Resilience

Emotional resourcefulness is the ability to stay grounded when life feels unstable. It is knowing how to reach within yourself for strength, peace, or creativity rather than collapse under pressure.

When disappointment comes, resourceful people don't say, *"I'm finished."* They ask, *"What can I learn?"* When plans fail, they pivot. When help is delayed, they improvise. When doors close, they build new ones.

Camels don't complain about the desert's harshness—they adjust and keep walking.

Likewise, resourceful people turn adversity into advantage.

Becoming a Resourceful Camel

To become a resourceful Camel is to develop the spiritual and practical discipline of making the most of what's in your hands. You may not have everything, but you have *something*—and that something can become a miracle when used with wisdom, Faith, and creativity.

Resourcefulness transforms ordinary people into extraordinary helpers. It says: "I may not have much, but I will not waste what I have." When you live that way, you empower others to see hope where they once saw limitation. You become proof that survival is possible in scarcity and that prosperity begins with perspective.

Reflection

- What resource (time, skill, relationship, or talent) have you been underestimating?
- How can you use what's already in your hand to help someone else?
- When faced with scarcity, do you focus on what's missing—or what's available?

Closing Thought

The desert doesn't reward those who complain about the heat; it rewards those who learn how to walk wisely through it. Resourcefulness is the spirit that turns wilderness into opportunity and adversity into innovation.

So, take inventory—not of what you lack, but of what you possess. Your next breakthrough may already be hidden in your hands. Camels remind us: survival isn't about abundance, it's about wisdom. And those who learn that lesson never truly run dry.

CHAPTER SEVEN

STRENGTH

Bearing the Weight of Others

"The world breaks everyone, and afterward,
some are strong at the broken places."
— Ernest Hemingway.

Strength is one of the most misunderstood virtues. Many see it as power, control, or dominance. But true strength, the kind that changes lives—is often silent. It's found in the person who keeps on loving after loss, serving without recognition, and standing firm when others fall away.

Camels teach us that kind of strength. They are not fast, fierce, or beautiful, yet they carry immense loads across impossible distances. Their power is quiet, dependable, and consistent. They remind us that real strength is not in how loud we roar but in how long we carry.

Strength, at its highest form, is not about overcoming others, it's about lifting them.

The Quiet Force That Sustains

The desert offers no shortcuts. The journey is long and weighty. Camels survive because they were built to bear burdens. They carry what others cannot, calmly and without complaint.

In the same way, strong people are those who shoulder Responsibility when the world becomes heavy. They are parents who hold families together through storms, mentors who stand firm when students falter, and friends who offer stability when life feels unstable.

Strength is not proven in comfort; it is revealed in crisis.

A Story of Faithful Strength

When Marcus's wife was diagnosed with a degenerative illness, everything changed overnight. Once a busy engineer, he set aside his career to care for her full-time. The weight was heavy—doctor visits, financial strain, emotional exhaustion—but Marcus carried it with grace.

Neighbors noticed his quiet devotion. Friends found hope in his faithfulness. He never called himself strong, yet his endurance became a source of strength for an entire community.

True strength doesn't draw attention—it draws others closer to hope.

Strength in Community: Shared Burdens

Strength multiplies when shared. Camels travel in caravans. When one tires, another adjusts pace. Their rhythm ensures the whole group survives. Likewise, no human being was created to carry everything alone. Our strength grows when it's joined with others.

There's power in the simple act of sharing burdens. A shared load becomes lighter. A shared struggle becomes survivable. When we choose to help someone carry their weight—emotionally, spiritually, or physically—we become instruments of healing.

A reflection of the divine design of community: strength is meant to circulate, not concentrate.

Strength and Compassion: The Perfect Balance

Strength without compassion becomes harsh. Compassion without strength becomes fragile. But when the two merge, lives are transformed.

Consider the story of *Benedicta's Wellness Seminar*. She had the passion to impact lives but lacked funds and support. When she was about to give up, someone reminded her, "Your Camels are coming." And they did. Helpers stepped in—some gave financially, others volunteered skills and time. Together, they lifted what she couldn't carry alone.

That is what strength looks like when shared: ordinary people combining Faith and compassion to accomplish extraordinary things.

Redefining Strength

Strength is not the absence of weakness. It is the choice to keep standing despite it. It's the mother who smiles while holding back tears, the leader who remains calm amid chaos, and the believer who still trusts after heartbreak.

Camels carry heavy loads not because it's easy but because it's necessary. Similarly, the strongest people are often those who never announce their pain. They carry others while quietly managing themselves.

Strength is not loud, it's loyal. Not boastful, it's steady. Not perfect, it's persistent.

Faith as the Source of Strength

For the person of Faith, strength is more than willpower, it's divine empowerment. Scripture says, *"The joy of the Lord is your strength."* (Nehemiah 8:10) This means strength flows not from striving but from resting in purpose.

When you draw strength from God, you stop depending on your own capacity. You become like a camel filled with reserves—able to walk farther than you thought possible, fueled by grace rather than grit.

Even outside the context of Faith, strength remains a spiritual principle: those who find meaning in what they carry always outlast those who carry without purpose.

How to Build Inner Strength

1. **Strengthen Your Mindset**: Focus on what you can control. Let go of what you can't. Strong minds create stable lives.
2. **Practice Emotional Stability**: Strength isn't emotionless, it's controlled emotion. Learn to pause, breathe, and respond rather than react.
3. **Carry Responsibility Willingly**: Don't fear the weight of purpose. The loads you carry shape your capacity.

4. **Care for Your Body and Spirit**: Physical, mental, and spiritual wellness are interconnected. A weak body drains courage; a nourished one renews it.
5. **Ask for Help When Needed**: True strength knows its limits. Admitting need is not weakness, it's wisdom.
6. **Keep Faith Alive**: Prayer, reflection, and gratitude build inner endurance. They remind you that you're carried even while carrying others.

Strength in the Face of Fear

In every desert season, fear whispers: *You won't make it.* But strength replies softly: *I already have.* Camels don't question the length of the journey; they trust their design. Likewise, you are built to withstand more than you realize. The same God who equipped the Camel for the desert equipped you for your destiny.

Your trials are not evidence of weakness—they are invitations to discover your depth.

A Story of History-Changing Strength

Harriet Tubman, once enslaved, escaped and then returned, again and again to rescue others through the Underground Railroad. Despite threats, exhaustion, and chronic illness, she carried dozens to freedom.

Her strength wasn't physical alone; it was moral, spiritual, and purposeful. When asked how she succeeded, she said, *"I never ran my train off the track, and I never lost a passenger."*

That's what divine strength looks like—faithful, fierce, and focused on lifting others.

Becoming a Strong Camel

To be a Camel is to be strong for the sake of others. It's to carry Responsibility without resentment, to serve without recognition, and to give without depletion.

Strength does not mean perfection. It means consistency to keep walking even when the path feels endless. When you carry others, you reveal God's heart. You become a living reminder that love is stronger than suffering and that faithfulness is more powerful than fear.

Reflection

- What load are you carrying right now that feels heavy, yet necessary?
- Who around you might need to borrow your strength for a season?
- How can you draw deeper strength, spiritually, emotionally, or relationally—rather than trying to push through alone?

Closing Thought

Strength is not measured by how much we can lift, but by how long we can love. It's not about domination, but devotion; not about winning but walking faithfully through the desert.

When life becomes heavy, remember the Camel's lesson: keep your pace, conserve your energy, and trust your design. You were built for this. And as you carry others, you'll discover the greatest truth of all— that the very act of lifting others is what keeps you strong.

CHAPTER EIGHT

LOYALTY
The Anchor of Connection

> *"Loyalty means nothing unless it has at its heart the absolute principle of self-sacrifice."*
> — Woodrow Wilson.

I n a world where commitments often fade with convenience, loyalty stands as one of the rarest and most powerful virtues. It is the bond that keeps relationships from unraveling and communities from breaking apart. Loyalty is not about blind allegiance — it is faithful presence, the decision to stand with others through change, difficulty, and time.

Camels teach us this kind of faithfulness. Once trained to travel with a caravan, they stay near their companions, returning to them even after long rests. They are dependable partners — steady, consistent, and devoted to the journey. Likewise, the strongest people are not those who make the biggest promises, but those who *keep showing up.*

Loyalty is the anchor of connection, and anchors do their best work unseen.

Faithful in the Long Journey

Loyalty is tested not in moments of comfort but in seasons of conflict and distance. It's easy to be faithful when everything is flourishing; true loyalty reveals itself when the journey becomes hard — when misunderstanding rises, when results are delayed, when no one else is watching.

Camels do not abandon their loads in the middle of the desert. They walk alongside others until the end. That's what loyal hearts do — they stay steady even when the scenery changes.

A Story of Unshakable Friendship

Scripture gives us one of the most profound portraits of loyalty in the friendship between David and Jonathan. Jonathan, the son of King Saul, had every reason to envy David. Yet instead of competing, he protected him. He risked his own life to defend David's destiny, even knowing that David would one day take the throne that by birth could have been his.

Jonathan's loyalty wasn't transactional — it was covenantal. It flowed from love, not leverage. His story reminds us that genuine loyalty often costs something — comfort, convenience, even reputation — but what it yields is priceless: trust that endures generations.

Loyalty as the Foundation of Trust

Trust is not built by talent; it is built by time. And loyalty is time made visible.

Every lasting relationship — between spouses, friends, leaders, or communities — rests on this foundation. Loyalty says, *"You can count on me when the crowd thins, when the applause fades, when life gets messy."*

In a culture that glorifies independence, loyalty feels countercultural. Yet, those who practice it experience depth that superficial relationships never reach. Loyalty turns ordinary connections into sacred bonds.

A Modern Story of Enduring Devotion

For forty years, Ms. Evelyn, a schoolteacher in a small town, poured herself into her students. Many came from broken homes, some from poverty, and others from discouragement. Long after her retirement, she still attended their graduations, weddings, and even funerals.

One day, one of her former students — now a senator — publicly thanked her, saying, "She never stopped believing in me, even when I didn't believe in myself."

Loyalty doesn't make headlines, but it leaves legacies. Ms. Evelyn's quiet devotion changed more futures than any single lesson she ever taught.

The Gift of Steadfast Presence

Loyalty is not about perfection — it's about *presence*. It's showing up even when it's inconvenient. It's listening without judgment. It's refusing to let temporary emotions erase permanent commitments.

In friendships, it looks like standing by someone through failure. In families, forgiveness keeps doors open. In leadership, it's about integrity that doesn't shift with the season.

Camels don't question the destination; they commit to the journey. That kind of faithfulness gives others the courage to keep walking.

Loyalty in Faith and Life

Faith traditions uphold loyalty as a reflection of divine character. The psalmist declared, *"Your faithfulness reaches to the skies."* (Psalm 36:5) God's loyalty to humanity is constant, undeserved, and unwavering — it is the model from which we learn.

For those outside of a faith context, loyalty remains equally vital. Psychologists agree that consistent, dependable relationships are essential for emotional well-being. People grow best in environments where love is not conditional but continuous.

Whether sacred or secular, loyalty nourishes stability — it gives the soul something to hold onto when everything else shifts.

How to Cultivate Loyalty

1. **Be Consistent**: Small acts of reliability build lifelong trust. Show up. Follow through. Keep your word.

2. **Value People Over Convenience**: Choose a relationship even when it's not easy. Loyalty sometimes requires sacrifice.
3. **Offer Grace, Not Perfection**: Stand by others when they fail. Loyalty is mercy in motion.
4. **Celebrate, Don't Compete**: Be genuinely happy for others' success. True loyalty claps from the sidelines.
5. **Stay Even When Unnoticed**: The deepest loyalty often happens in silence, without recognition or reward.

A Legacy of Loyal Friendship

In the early 1900s, two visionaries — George Washington Carver and Henry Ford — formed an unlikely friendship that crossed racial and social barriers. Ford admired Carver's brilliance and humility; Carver valued Ford's generosity and curiosity.

Their bond endured for decades. In Carver's old age, Ford even built a special elevator in his company headquarters so his friend could visit comfortably. Their loyalty defied the prejudices of their time, proving that commitment born of respect can outlive cultural boundaries.

Loyalty is a bridge — and those who build it make the world a kinder place.

Becoming a Loyal Camel

To be a Camel is to be trustworthy. It's to carry relationships as sacred cargo, not disposable conveniences. Loyal Camels are the ones who stay when others leave, who keep on believing when others doubt, who keep walking beside someone even when the desert gets long.

Loyalty doesn't just hold others up; it holds *you* together. It roots you in integrity and reminds you that real success is measured not by how many people follow you, but by how many can rely on you.

Reflection

- Who in your life has shown you loyalty when you least deserve it?
- Where might your commitment need strengthening — in Faith, family, or friendship?
- How can you be an anchor for someone else this week?

Closing Thought

The desert winds will always shift, but loyalty keeps the caravan moving forward. It is the invisible thread that holds purpose, relationships, and communities together.

So, choose to stay. Choose to stand. Choose to be faithful even when it costs you something because in the end, the world remembers not those who walked away, but those who walked beside. Loyalty is the love that lasts — the anchor of every meaningful connection.

CHAPTER NINE

CALMNESS
Stability in the Storm

"Peace is not the absence of conflict, but the presence of God in the midst of it."
— Unknown.

There is a strength that does not shout, push, or struggle. It simply stands still. Calmness is that strength. It is the composure that holds you together when everything else falls apart. It is the still water beneath the surface waves — deep, undisturbed, and quietly powerful.

In every desert, storms come without warning. The heat intensifies, the winds shift, the sands rise. Those who panic waste energy; those who stay calm survive. The Camel, once again, teaches us: in crisis, steadiness saves.

Calmness does not mean denial or detachment. It means being centered enough to act wisely when others react emotionally. It is not passivity — it is power under control.

The Power of Stillness

In a noisy and anxious world, calmness is revolutionary. It is the difference between responding and reacting, between discernment and distraction.

The truly calm person does not feel fear, but one who refuses to be ruled by it. Camels don't outrun storms; they endure them. They kneel, face the wind, and wait for the worst to pass. When others collapse from exhaustion, the calm endure through patience.

Calmness gives you that same posture. It's the quiet courage to kneel instead of panic, to pause instead of exploding, to breathe instead of break.

A Story of Poised Strength

During a natural disaster, a young rescue worker named Caleb was assigned to a flooded district. Roads were impassable, and communication lines were down. Panic spread fast. But Caleb refused to lose composure.

He organized neighbors into small rescue teams, coordinated children's evacuations, and kept everyone focused. Days later, a journalist asked how he managed to stay calm amid chaos. He said, *"If I panic, others will too. Someone has to be the still point."*

That is the essence of calmness: it stabilizes others. Like an anchor, it doesn't stop the storm — but it keeps the ship from drifting away.

Calmness and Resilience

Calmness is not the absence of motion but the mastery of emotion.

It is the soil in which resilience grows. When panic reigns, wisdom hides, but when calmness rules, clarity returns.

Every great leader, parent, counselor, or believer learns this: storms will test your calm. If you can stay composed when others crumble, you become a source of strength. If you can speak peace when others shout fear, you carry healing in your presence.

Camels embody this balance. Their steady pace through chaos is a metaphor for spiritual and emotional maturity. They move forward with patience, unaffected by external noise.

Faith and the Practice of Peace

Faith gives calmness its deepest root. It reminds us that peace is not found in control, but in trust. Jesus slept through a storm while His disciples panicked. The lesson was not that the storm wouldn't come — but that inner peace can remain even while the winds rage.

Isaiah wrote, *"You will keep him in perfect peace, whose mind is stayed on You."* (Isaiah 26:3) That is calmness — not the absence of trouble, but the presence of focus. When your heart anchors in divine stability, external chaos loses power over you.

Even for those outside of Faith, calmness is still a spiritual posture. It's an act of alignment — choosing perspective over panic, wisdom over worry, grace over anger.

A Modern Example: The CEO Who Led Through Crisis

When global markets crashed, the company Arcadia Technologies faced bankruptcy. Employees panicked; investors fled. But the CEO, Leah Torres, made a counterintuitive choice — she didn't rush.

Instead, she gathered her team daily, spoke transparently, and reminded them of their shared purpose. Her calm leadership restored confidence. Within months, the company stabilized and rebuilt. Later, she reflected, *"The calmest voice in the room often determines the outcome."*

Her composure saved not just company but countless livelihoods. Calmness is influence at its quietest and most effective.

How to Cultivate Calmness

1. Practice Centered Breathing: Calmness often begins with breath. When emotions rise, breathe slowly and deeply. It resets your body before your mind follows.

2. Create Quiet Spaces: Spend intentional time in silence each day. Calmness grows in the soil of stillness.

3. Guard Your Thoughts: What you focus on multiply. Replace panic narratives with faith-filled or hopeful ones.

4. Respond, Don't React: Before speaking or deciding, pause. The calm response often prevents unnecessary storms.

5. Keep Perspective: Most storms don't last forever. Remind yourself: this too shall pass.

6. Anchor in Faith or Purpose: Calmness flows from conviction — the belief that something greater is holding you steady.

Calmness in Relationships

Calmness is contagious. When one person remains steady, others find security.

In relationships, calmness diffuses conflict. It invites understanding rather than escalation. A calm parent teaches stability. A calm spouse models maturity. A calm friend offers safety.

Camels don't just survive the desert—they help others survive it. Likewise, your calm presence becomes a gift that carries others through their chaos.

The Discipline of Inner Peace

Inner peace requires intentional maintenance. It's not automatic; it's cultivated through spiritual, mental, and emotional practices.

- **Prayer and reflection** quiet the noise within.
- **Gratitude** redirects focus from what's missing to what's working.
- **Boundaries** protect your calm by managing energy and expectations.

Camels stop to rest before exhaustion overtakes them. They understand that renewal is survival. You must do the same — refill your peace before life drains it.

Becoming a Calm Camel

To be a Camel is to walk with composure through life's extremes. It's to carry grace under pressure, to think clearly when others can't, and to trust deeply when outcomes remain uncertain.

Calm people don't control every situation — they control themselves. That is their secret strength. When you master calmness, you not only endure storms; you guide others through them. Your peace becomes their path.

Reflection

- What situations most easily disrupt your calmness, and why?
- How can you build daily habits that preserve inner peace?
- Who around you need the gift of your calm presence today?

Closing Thought

Calmness is not weakness. It is wisdom at rest. It is the quiet authority that says, *"I trust the process. I will not be moved."* The desert will bring storms — but storms will pass. The calm traveler keeps walking, steady and sure.

And when the winds finally die down, it is the calm soul who sees clearly enough to lead others forward.

Be that Camel. Stable, grounded, unshaken, because peace, not panic, is true proof of strength.

CHAPTER TEN

BECOMING A CAMEL

The Call to Empower Others

"We rise by lifting others."
— Robert Ingersoll

Every journey lead to a point of transformation — that moment when you realize your trials were never only about you. They were training. The deserts you crossed, the lessons you learned, the storms you endured — they were all preparation to make you stronger for someone else. That's what it means to become a Camel: not just to receive help, but to *become* help.

The Camel is more than a symbol of endurance; it is a calling — a picture of purpose lived out through resilience, patience, adaptability, resourcefulness, strength, loyalty, and calmness. You are not just walking through life's desert — you are called to make the journey easier for others who come behind you.

From Receiver to Giver

Every person begins their journey in need of others.

We all rely on mentors, parents, friends, and even strangers who show up at crucial moments. They are the "Camels" sent to help us cross difficult terrains. But at some point, the baton must pass. The strength poured into us must now flow through us.

Life's greatest fulfillment is found not in comfort but in contribution.

When you start to carry others — through your wisdom, your kindness, your presence — you complete the cycle of resilience. You become part of the divine network that sustains the world.

Camels that carry nothing soon lose purpose. Humans who live only for themselves soon lose their sense of meaning.

A Story of Passing Strength Forward

After losing her job during an economic downturn, Lydia spent months struggling with self-doubt and fear. During that season, a neighbor encouraged her to volunteer at a community center. She reluctantly agreed. There, she met others facing similar hardship.

As Lydia began mentoring young women searching for direction, she noticed something remarkable — her confidence returned. The same encouragement that once carried her through dark days was now flowing out of her.

Years later, she said, *"Helping others healed me."*

That is the secret of transformation: the moment you begin lifting others, you yourself are lifted.

Empowerment Through Example

Becoming a Camel is not about having all the answers. It's about walking with others through their uncertainty, reminding them that they are not alone.

Empowerment is not a lecture; it's a lifestyle. It's expressed through presence, consistency, and compassion. When people watch how you handle life — with grace in difficulty and calm in crisis — you become a living message of hope.

In a world full of noise, your resilience will speak louder than your words.

The Ripple Effect of Helping

One act of kindness can travel farther than you imagine. The person you encourage today may go on to lift ten others. The child you mentor may one day lead a nation. The colleague you steady may rediscover purpose and, in turn, restore others.

Camels carry supplies that sustain entire caravans — water, food, life itself. Likewise, your strength carries more than you realize. The world may never record your name, but eternity remembers the lives touched by your endurance and grace.

The Leadership of Service

True leadership is servanthood. The greatest leaders — in Faith, business, or family — are those who understand that to lead is to carry.

They use their influence not to elevate themselves but to elevate others. They build people, not just projects. They create legacy through lifted lives.

Every quality explored in this book — resilience, patience, adaptability, endurance, resourcefulness, strength, loyalty, calmness — is preparation for this. These virtues refine you not merely for survival, but for *service*.

Camels are not admired for their beauty, but for their contribution. They exist to carry, to deliver, to help the journey succeed. That is the model for meaningful living.

Faith and the Calling to Carry

Faith reminds us that we are all carriers of grace. The apostle Paul wrote, *"Bear one another's burdens, and so fulfill the law of Christ."* (Galatians 6:2)

That is what it means to be a Camel in the Kingdom — to use your life to lift others, to embody God's compassion in practical form. Every time you show patience, offer kindness, or stay faithful in service, you are living out this divine design.

And even outside the language of Faith, this truth remains: humanity survives because people choose to care, to help, to carry one another forward. That is the unseen force that holds societies together.

How to Live as a Camel

1. Stay Available: You don't have to be perfect to be useful. You only have to be willing. Show up when others need you.

2. Be an Encourager: Speak life into weary hearts. A word of hope can be the water someone needs to keep walking.

3. Share Your Story: Someone needs to know how you made it through. Transparency multiplies strength.

4. Invest in the Next Generation: Pour into others what was once poured into you. Legacies are built through teaching, not just through achievement.

5. Keep Growing: The best Camels are always learning. Continue developing your character and capacity to serve more effectively.

A Modern Example: The Mentor Who Multiplied Hope

A retired nurse named Mr. Ade began volunteering at a youth center after decades of service. Every week, he met with young adults struggling with purpose, teaching them life skills and resilience.

One student said, "He made me believe I could endure anything."

Years later, those same young adults started a foundation in his honor — *The Camel Network* — to continue helping others through mentorship and education.

One person's faithfulness became a movement. That's the ripple of a Camel's life.

Becoming the Miracle You Once Needed

At some point, each of us cried out for help — and someone came.

Now, it's our turn to be that answer for someone else.

Becoming a Camel means realizing that your life is a resource — that your resilience was never wasted, your patience was never pointless, and your endurance was never unseen. It was all shaping you into someone others can lean on.

You are the proof that helps come — that people do show up — that deserts can be crossed.

Reflection

- Who carried you through your most difficult seasons, and how can you honor them by carrying others?
- What strengths or lessons have your pain given you that could now empower someone else?
- What one action can you take this week to "be the Camel" in another person's journey?

Closing Thought

To become a Camel is to embrace the sacred calling of connection — not just to receive help, but to become it. It is to walk through life not as one who seeks applause, but as one carrying purpose.

The Camels are indeed coming — but they are also *rising*. They are people like you and me, choosing every day to live with resilience, compassion, and grace.

And as they walk, they carry the world forward — one life, one act of faithfulness, one desert crossing at a time.

EPILOGUE
The Legacy of the Journey

Every generation needs its Camels — men and women who carry strength where there is weakness, peace where there is panic, and love where there is loss. The desert of life will never disappear. It will always demand endurance, courage, and hope. But so long as people are willing to lift others, the world will never run dry.

You may not realize it yet, but someone's survival depends on your steadiness.

Your resilience permits them to keep walking. Your calm teaches them peace. Your Faith inspires their courage. You are part of a sacred caravan — a movement of hope, quietly crossing the sands of life with grace.

So, lift your head, steady your heart, and keep walking. Your journey matters — not just for you, but for everyone who will one day say, *"Because of your strength, I made it through."*

AUTHOR'S REFLECTION

As I wrote these pages, I found myself learning from the very lessons I sought to share. Every season of struggle became a teacher, every helper a symbol, every challenge a doorway to deeper resilience.

If this book reminds you of anything, let it be this: you are stronger than you think, and your life carries meaning beyond what you can see.

May you never underestimate the quiet miracle of showing up — the power of patience, the wisdom of adaptability, the grace of loyalty, and the peace of calmness.

May you live as one who not only finds strength but gives it freely.

Because when you become a Camel, you don't just survive in the desert —

You help others find their way home.

— **Olu Ojeikere**

ABOUT THE AUTHOR

Olu Ojeikere is a communicator, author, and teacher dedicated to helping people live with purpose, clarity, and courage. He blends Faith, psychology, and practical wisdom to inspire resilience and meaningful connection.

His previous books, *Principles for a Year-Round Winning Life: 365 Daily Wisdom Nuggets* and *Everyday Wisdom: Time-Tested Principles for Daily Living*, have touched readers across cultures. With *The Camels Are Coming*, Ojeikere continues his mission to empower others to rise, rebuild, and remain strong through life's changing seasons.

www.ingramcontent.com/pod-product-compliance
Lightning Source LLC
Chambersburg PA
CBHW070057100426

42740CB00013B/2863

* 9 7 8 1 7 3 4 3 9 9 1 6 5 *